LIFE OF
GENERAL JOHN TIPTON
AND
EARLY INDIANA HISTORY

INTRODUCTION.

During the summer of 1905, the writer of this book was in the omce of Dr. H. G. Read, when the latter asked the question, "What great things did General Tipton do that our County and City and other Counties and Cities are named for him, and so little said of him in history?" In the conversation that followed, bits of information was gleaned until the subject became of considerable interest. At that time the Doctor was the President of the Tipton Literary and Suffrage Club, and he suggested that a paper on the life of General John Tipton be prepared and read before the club. Acting upon this suggestion, the program committee set apart a "Tipton Night" and Mrs. Sam Matthews was selected to prepare and read a paper on the subject. After careful re-search and much labor, she prepared and read a most valuable and interesting paper. It aroused considerable discussion and much information was derived. The members of the club became so enthused that they conceived the idea of raising a fund for the purpose of erecting a monument, or tablet or a painting to the memory of the man for whom the County and City were named. Committees were appointed to adopt a plan for a monument. Those who took the initiative and gave life to the movement were Dr. and Mrs. H. G. Read, Dan and Mrs. Waugh, George H. and Mrs. Gifford. Mrs. George Teter, Mrs. Sam Matthews, Mrs. W. L. Berryman, Mrs. W. H. Ogan, Mrs. E. H.Shirk, Mrs. Dr. Dickey, Mrs. William Standerford, M. W. Pershing and others whose names cannot just now be recalled. For some time the subject was more or less discussed, but no definite plans were matured until during the last summer, when Prof. C. F. Patterson, Superintendent of the City Schools and L. D. Summers, County Superintendent of Schools, heard of the movement and they suggested that as the project was of historic importance, that it be brought before the public schools and that it be made a County affair. This was thought advisable and it was made a special feature before the County Teachers' Institute. An address was made before the Teachers' Institute, giving a brief account of the life and achievements of General Tipton, from which the teachers throughout the County became deeply interested and it was decided that we have a "Tipton Day" on October 25, when a program was rendered in honor of the great General for whom our County was named. It was also decided that a history should be written especially devoted to the life of the General and the undersigned was selected to write this volume.

The history and biography of General Tipton has been fully written for the first time in this volume, very much of it never having been in print before. To secure this material difficult re-search was made, and considerable correspondence with many people, who had some relic about their homes as a reminder of the deeds of General Tipton. Old books, old pamphlets, old magazines, old newspapers, and old letters were hunted up and read with little bits of information gathered here and there, we are enabled to produce a volume pertaining to Indiana history and the life of a man whom historians have paid little attention. For a great deal of this material the writer is indebted to Lieutenant-Governor Th. Hugh Miller and George Price, of Columbus, B. F. Lawrence, managing editor of the Indianapolis Star. Hon. Dan. McDonald, of Plymouth, A. O. Reser and Thomas E. Burt, of LaFayette, the latter loaning us several of the illustrations appearing in this edition. We are under special obligations to Reed Beard, of Lafayette, author of the "Battle of Tippecanoe," for the use of maps and charts, also to M. W. Phillips, of LaFayette for valuable information heretofore unpublished together with a letter written by Judge Isaac Naylor, of Crawfordsville, who was in the battle of Tippecanoe and was one of the first to arrive at Pigeon Roost after the massacre. This letter was found quite recently among some old papers in the possession of the Judge's daughter.

The object in the publication of this work is that valuable historic events in the State of Indiana may be preserved and that deeds performed and sacrifices made by Gen. John Tipton may become more gen-

LIFE OF GENERAL JOHN TIPTON AND EARLY INDIANA HISTORY

BY

M. W. PERSHING

ISBN: 978-93-5128-731-5(HB)

First Published in 1900
Indian Reprint in 2017

Published by

Kalpaz Publications
C-30, Satyawati Nagar,
Delhi – 110052
E-mail: kalpaz@hotmail.com
Website: kalpazpublications.com
Ph.: +91-9212142040

Cataloging in Publication Data—DK
Courtesy: D.K. Agencies (P) Ltd. <docinfo@dkagencies.com>

Pershing, M. W. (Marvin W.), 1849- **author.**
Life of General John Tipton and early Indiana history / by M.W. Pershing.
pages cm
"First published in 1900"--Title page verso.
ISBN 9789351287315 (HB)

1. Tipton, John, 1786-1839. 2. Generals—United States—Biography. 3. Indiana—History. I. Title.

F526.P47 2017 DDC 977.203092 23

erally known. The net proceeds of the sale of this book is to be entirely devoted to creating a fund toward the erection of a monument to the memory of the man who was a citizen, a statesman, an Indian fighter and a history maker. The writer takes great pleasure in dedicating this volume to the Public Schools and the Citizens of Tipton County and hopes that it may encourage a greater interest in the earlier history of the State and create a patriotic sentiment for those who did so much for American civilization.

Life of General John Tipton.

The Tipton family is of Irish lineage. Joshua Tipton, the father of the subject of this sketch was born in Maryland. In early manhood he removed to Sevier County, East Tennessee, then known as the territory of Franklin, and there he was married to Jeanette Shields. Joshua Tipton was an Indian fighter and soon became a leader in public affairs of Tennessee.

There are stirring stories of a fued between the Tipton family and the Sevier's (for whom the County was named.) It was waged with characteristic Southern heat and the bitter vindictiveness which has made each a tragic element in the history of so many communities in the young South. This fued ended on April 16, 1798, in the death of Joshua Tipton, apparently at the hands of a marauding band of Cherokee Indians. But it is unwritten history that the assassination was arranged and timed by the Seviers. It was under such conditions and such influences that John Tipton was born, August 14, 1786. He was seven years of age at the time of his father's death. When he was twenty-one years of age he moved with his mother and family to Indiana, settling near Bringley's Ferry, in Harrison County. Here he was the chief support of the family, and by repairing guns and working as a farm hand, he was enabled to buy a farm of fifty acres. His mother died at Seymour in 1827.

John Tipton was not in the new territory long before his qualities as a leader became recognized. The constant fear of hostile Indians, horse thieves, counterfeiters and river desperadoes kept the settlers on

W. H. Harrison

the alert and Tipton was found to be a man that could be relied upon as an indefatigable enemy to Indians and evil doers.

In June, 1809, the Sheriff of Harrison County formed a company of mounted riflemen for active service in Indian warfares. Of this company, "The Yellow Jackets," so called from the peculiar color of their uniforms, John Tipton became a member. On September 12, 1811, the company was marching on general orders of Gov. Harrison to rendezvous at Vincennes. This campaign was made against the hostile Indians on the Wabash River and contributes an important chapter of the war of 1812. This expedition, while apparently not important in itself, lies at the foundation of a mighty fact in our development, for the "Battle of Tippecanoe" led the English to see that their Indian allies were not to be relied upon, and they therefore withdrew from the alliance and thus made it possible for the United States to control the four great States of the Middle West.

During this expedition John Tipton kept a daily journal, the only one kept by any one during that long march. The following are a few extracts from this diary, the original of which is now on file with the Historical Society at Indianapolis. It will be observed that Tipton was an uneducated man, though there is method and system in all his records:

> "thirsday, 12, of September, 1811, when the company departed from Corydon to Sunday, 24, November, when the stragling remnant of the company returned."
>
> "An encompt of the march and Encampment of the riflemen of harrison county, commanded by Capt. Spier Spencer, consisted of 47 men besides officers in Company with R. m. heath with 22 men."

The journal gives particulars of each day and the doings of the writer. It appears from the records that he was always ready for everything that came up. It is written with evident modesty, but his ability and adaptability assert themselves continually. Standing post, scouting, hunting lost horses, repairing guns of his company, acting as a spy, hunting game for his mess and making himself generally useful, thus he was in close touch with his comrades. Here are a few more extracts that are very interesting:

> "thirsday 12 of September 1811 Left Corry-

> don at 3 oclock marched six miles to governor harrisons mill and Encampt had our horses in posture."
>
> "12. marched 34 miles and on the way was joined by Capt. Berry with 20 men and Encampt at a good Spring."
>
> "14. marched 3 miles and Encampt at the half moon Spring was joined by Capt. baggs with a troop of horses and in the Evening by Col bartholomew with 120 melitia from Clark County."

It must be remembered that John Tipton never went to school and his ability to write at all was through his own efforts and his desire to become a useful man. From his diary we gather a report of the movements of the army. On Wednesday, November 18, 1811, the army reached Vincennes, where the troops were mustered, and general orders issued by Gov. Harrison on September 22, and Major J. H. Daviess was appointed in command of all the dragoons. Tipton was appointed Ensign of the company to which he belonged and it was ordered as a detached corps of mounted volunteers.

The army under the command of Gov. Harrison moved from Vincennes on September 26, and on October 3, arrived at Terre Haute. The events of the next few weeks are here given in Tipton's own language:

> "thirsday 3d. marched at 9 four of our horses missing the men left to hunt them marched one mile Came to tare-hott an oald indian village on east side of wabash on high land near a Large Prarie Peach and aple trees growing."

In this vicinity the Indians had been very troublesome, killing many settlers, stealing horses and cattle and driving the whites into Vincennes. Gov. Harrison had promised the fugitives whom he met at Vincennes that he would make a decisive campaign against the Indians. After a few days march from Terre Haute a halt was made and the army engaged in the building of a fort, which was named Fort Harrison and was completed October 28. After the fort was completed Harrison sent some Delaware Chiefs to the Prophet on a mission of peace, offering

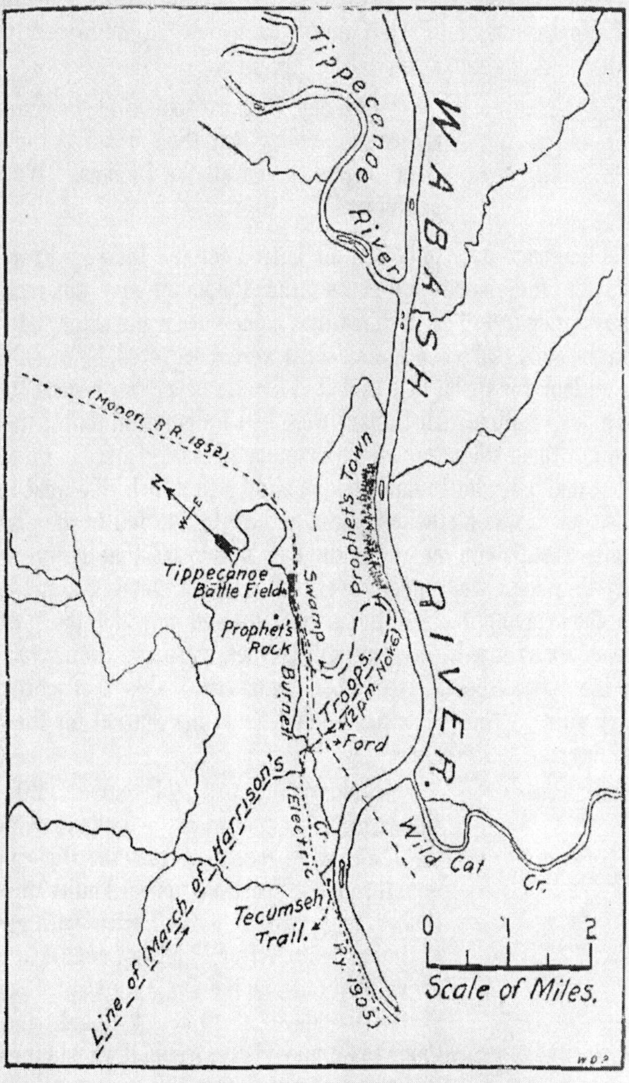
WABASH RIVER.
Tippecanoe River
(Monon R.R. 1852)
Prophet's Town
Tippecanoe Battle Field
Prophet's Rock
Swamp
Burnet
Troops (12 p.m. Nov. 6)
Ford
Wild Cat Cr.
Cr.
(Electric Ry. 1905)
Tecumseh Trail.
Line of March of Harrison's
0 1 2
Scale of Miles.

terms of surrender, but the Prophet treated the proposition with scorn. Upon receiving this refusal the army marched toward Prophet's Town. The army was composed of about nine hundred and ten, embracing about two hundred and fifty regular troops, sixty volunteers from Kentucky and about six hundred Indiana volunteers. On October 31 the army passed Racoon Creek and crossed the Wabash River at the present site of Montazuma, in Park County, of which Tipton wrote in his journal:

> "thirsday 31st we took a north cours up the east of valley and then crosst to the west with orders to kill all the Indians. We saw fine news."

His language here indicates his hatred for the Indian. From the fact that the Indians had killed his father the young man was ready to obey any order to kill all Indians that came within his sight. He was ever on the alert and when Indian signs were discovered, he was always on the outlook for them. It is said that Tipton never saw a good Indian except a dead Indian. All Indians were bad Indians and that it was his duty to kill them whenever an opportunity presented itself. He was a sure shot and when an Indian came in sight a flint-lock rifle went to his shoulder, there was a crack of a gun and an Indian fell to the ground. So deadly was his aim that when the Red Man heard that he was in the vicinity they kept well under cover and avoided meeting him.

As the army approached the historic ground on which the battle of Tippecanoe was fought his journal becomes more interesting, and as this is the only authentic account of the march, makes it of more than ordinary value. The following is taken from his journal for the next several days:

> "Sunday the 3rd (November, 1811) a cloudy day. we moved eary. our Company on the Right wing today. Crosst the Big vermillion, through a Prarie six miles, 3 miles through timber, then through a wet Prairie with groves of timber in it. After 18 miles Camped in Rich grove of timber in the Prairie. Capt. Spencer very sick today. at 10 oclock tonight the aid Came to Camp and orec a subaltern and the men to Parade at the Governor's tent. at 4 in the

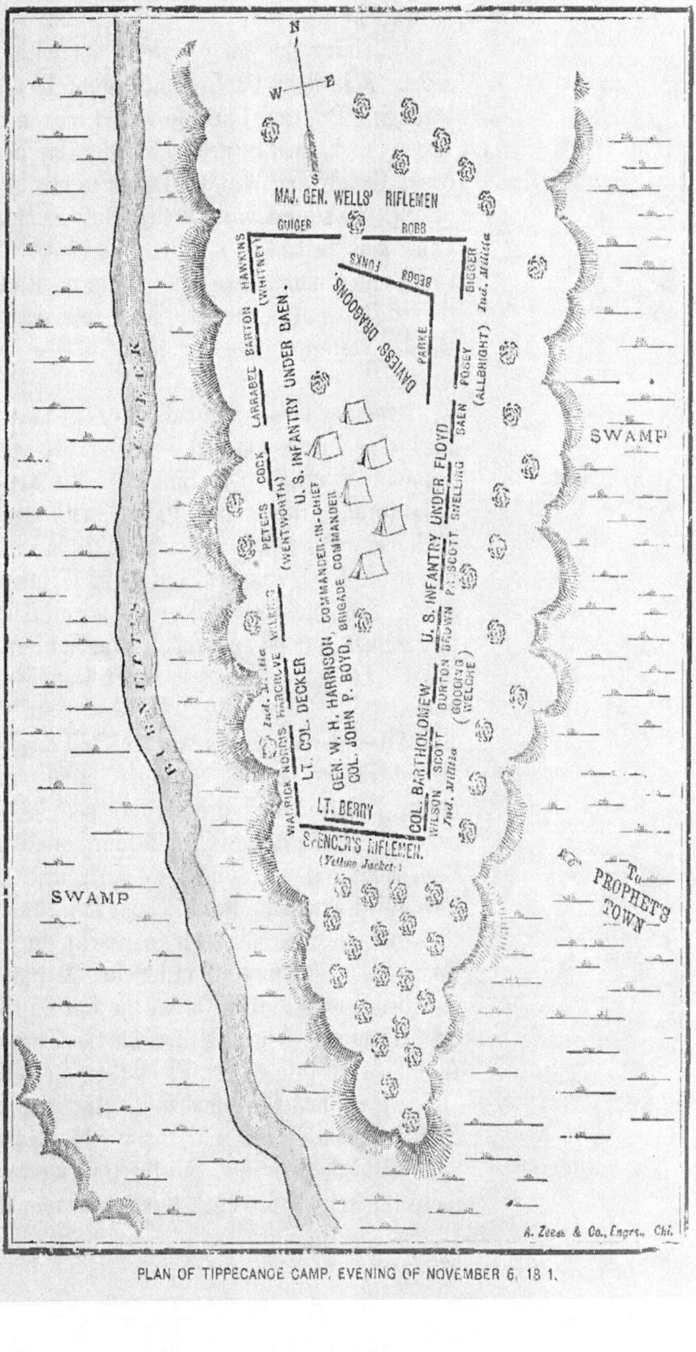

PLAN OF TIPPECANOE CAMP, EVENING OF NOVEMBER 6, 18 1.

morning I was ordered out. my Company maid up. a gun fired while I am writing at eleven oclock."

"Monday the 4th. I went out with my scout. Joined by Capt. Prince, went 18 miles through a Prairie. Came to Pine Creek, a fine Large Creek, then turned back. the Day being could, Cloudy and Windy. Began to rain at 11 oclock. we stoped to make fire, But the armey Came and we had to leve it. We crosst Pine Creek and Campd. two gun fired at 8. it Continewd Raing at intervales. I had one quart of whisky yesterday and one today of the Contractor."

"tuesday the 5. a Cloudy day. we mooved Earley. a Lieutenant and 5 men sent to scout. Came to the armey. no Sine Seed We went 6 miles through timber then Prairie, with groves of timber and a number of small lakes in it. an alarm maid. I was Sent out with 17 men to Scout. Seed nothing. a Deer and a wolf Killed in the line. Campd on a Small Branch after 18 miles. the guns fired last night wounded a horse."

"Wednesday the 6. A vary Cold day, we moved Earley. Scout Sent out. they came back. had seed indian Sine. we marched as usuel till 12. Our Spies Caught four horses and Seed some indians. found we ware near the Celebrated Prophet's town. Stopt in a Prairie. the foot throwd all their napsacks in the waggons. we found in order for A Battle. marched 2 miles. then formd the line of Battle. we marched in five lines on the extreme Right. Went into a Corn Field, then up to the above town and Surrounded it. the met us. Pled for Peace. the said the would give us Satisfac in the morning. all the time we ware there the kept hollowing. this town is on the west side of Wabash—miles above vincinnes, on the second Bank, neat built, about 2 hundred yards from the river. this is the main town, but it is Scattering a mile long, all the way a fine Corn field, after the above moovement we moovd one mild farther up. Campd in tim(ber) between a Creek and a Prairie af(ter) Crossing a fine Creek and marching 11 miles."

"thirsday the 7. agreeable to their Promise Last night we were answered by the fireing of guns and the Shawines Braking into our tents. a Blood Combat Took Plaice Precisely 15 minutes Before five in the morning. which Lasted 2 hours and 20 minutes, of a Continewel fireing whil maney time mixed among the indians So that we Could not tell them, indians and our men apart. they kept up a fireing on three sides of us and took our tent from the guard fire. Our men fought brave and by the timely help of Capt Cook with a Company of infantry we maid a Charge and Drove them out of our timber across the Prairie. our Losst and Killd and wounded was 179. and their graiter than ours. among the Dead was our Capt Spier Spencer and firs Lieut memahon and Capt Berrey that had Been attachd to our Company, and 5 more Kild Dead and 15 wounded. after the indians gave ground we Burried our Dead. among the Kentucians was Killd may J. Owins and may J. Davies badly wounded and a number of others. in all Killd and wounded was 179 but no Company Suffered like ours. we then held an Election for Officers. I was Elected Capt. Saml flanagan first Lieut and Jacob Zenor Second Liet. and Philip Bell Ensign. we then built Breast work, our men in much confusion in our rear.

flower been too small and all our beevs lost Last night onley a half Rations of whisky and

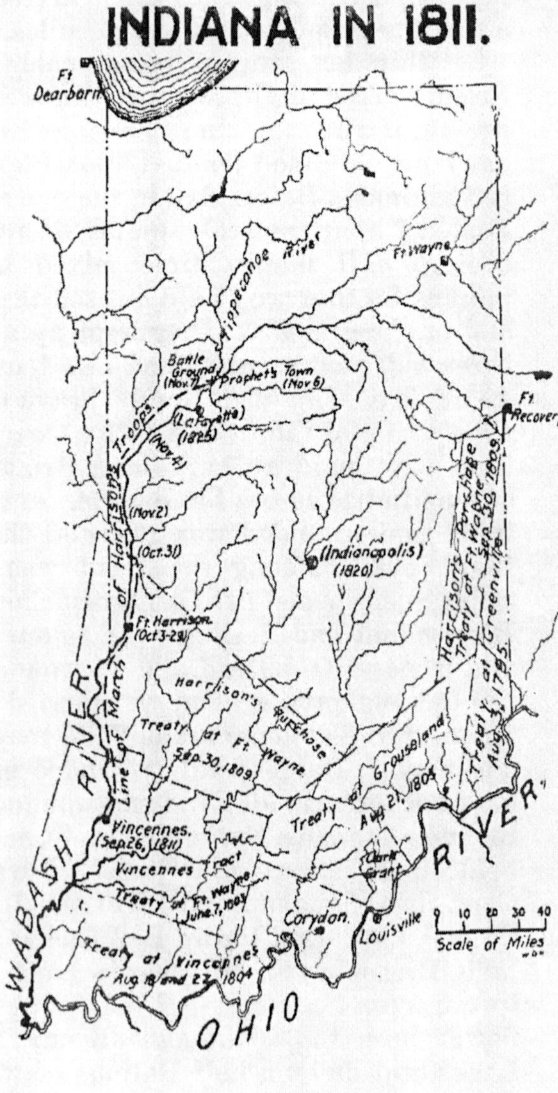
INDIANA IN 1811.
Ft Dearborn
Tippecanoe River
Ft Wayne
Battle Ground (Nov.7)
Prophet's Town (Nov 6)
Ft. Recovery
(Lafayette) (1825)
Line of March of Harrison's Troops
(Nov 4)
(Nov 2)
(Oct. 31)
(Indianapolis) (1820)
Harrison's Purchase Treaty at Ft. Wayne Sep. 30, 1809
Ft. Harrison. (Oct 3-29)
Treaty at Greenville Aug. 3, 1795.
Harrison's Purchase Treaty at Ft. Wayne Sep. 30, 1809.
Treaty at Grouseland Aug 21, 1805
WABASH RIVER.
Vincennes. (Sep 26, 1811)
Vincennes Tract
Treaty at Ft. Wayne June 7, 1803
Clark Grant
RIVER
Corydon.
Louisville
0 10 20 30 40
Scale of Miles
Treaty at Vincennes Aug. 18 and 27, 1804
OHIO

no corn for our horses. my horse Killd. I got memahons to ride. 37 of them had been Killd wounded and Lost. I had one quart of whis(ky) last night."

"friday the 8th. a Cloudy day and Last night was also wet and cold. we Lay all night at our Breast work without fire. in the morning Spies Sent out found the indians had left their town. the horsemen was all sent to burn their town. to wet went ann found grait deal of Corn. and some Dead indians in the houses. Loaded 6 waggons with Corn, and Burnt what Estimated at 2 thousand Bushels. 9 of our men Died last night."

The Indians not returning after the battle, the army moved toward Vincennes. Tipton continued to keep his diary, but there was nothing of an unusual character occurred upon the return trip. After the discharge of the volunteer soldiers at Vincennes, the following entry is made in the journal:

"Sunday Nov 24th, a Cloudy and Rainy morning, we mooved Early. Come to Corrydon at half past 10. took Breakfast, mooved up to Coonrods, found my Lieut and sick man. Staid 2 hours had my horses fed, got some whisky, met one of my neighbors, mooved again and at 10 oclock got safe Home after a Campain of 74 days. (signed) John Tipton."

Following this is a foot note which completes the journal for this campaign and closes the incidents of the war with the Indians and the battle of Tippecanoe:

"this Day Book Kept During the Campain in the Year 1811, wherein his Ex-Cellency Governor Harrison was Commander in Chief and Col. J. B. Boyd of the 4th United States Reigement was Second in Command. Everything herein stated the Subscriber holds his self Ready to make appear to Bee Fact from the best information Could Bee as it was duly Kept by his self."

Oliver H. Smith in his book, "Early Trials and Sketches," in writing of the battle of Tippecanoe and the achievements of John Tipton, has the following to say:

"A dark night came on. It was probable that the Prophet would strike that night, if at all, the men lay on their arms, the officers at their respective command. 'Hark!' the sound of rifles. The sentinels were either shot or driven in, the attack was made over the east and west banks of the high lands, bordering the prairies. The moment the alarm was given, every soldier was on his feet and the mounted officers in their saddles. Gen. Harrison ran to the post where he left his gray mare. Finding Major Owens bay horse he mounted, leaving the gray for the Major if he could find her. The General dashed down to where he heard the firing, rode up to Capt. Spencer's position at the point of a high ground around which the prairies met, where the enemy had made the first attack—deadly in effect. There stood the brave Ensign, John Tipton, and a few of the surviving men of the company. In a loud voice Gen. Harrison called out:

"'Where is the Captain of this company?'

"To which John Tipton answered, 'Dead, Sir."

"'Where is the First Lieutenant?'

"'He is dead, Sir.'

"'Where is the Second Lieutenant?'

"'He is dead.'

"'Where is the Ensign?'

"'I am here," answered Tipton.

"'Stand fast, my brave fellow, stand fast, and I will get relief for you in a few minutes.'"

General Harrison always spoke of Ensign Tipton as the coolest and bravest officer he had in his command. Standing there with sword drawn, facing the oncoming Indians, looking at death and seeing his comrades falling all about him, he held the position until relief came and the Indians were driven back. The day was saved. The great Tecumseh federation had failed and the great Prophet's heart was broken. It was Tipton that stood between savagery and civilization. It was he that made it possible that the power of the Indian was broken and the great states of Indiana, Illinois, Michigan and Wisconsin freed of hostile Indians and brought under the domination of Anglo-Saxon government. The British government bowed to the inevitable and withdrew its support from the Indians. The Prophet Tecumseh went to Detroit where he severed his relations with the British government

INDIAN WAR DANCE.

[From Fam us Frontiersmen, Pioneers and Scouts; published by W. H. Harrison, Jr., Publishing Co., Chicago.]

and went to Canada, where he lived the life of an exile, hated and despised by both whites and reds, and died a miserable death alone and unattended.

In 1839 the bones of the soldiers that fell in the battle of Tippecanoe, which had been disinterred by the Indians for revenge and robbery, were gathered together and buried again. The battle grounds was purchased by Gen. Tipton, the deed being recorded at Crawfordsville. After holding it a few years he donated it to the State of Indiana.

The Legislature had passed an act commanding the Governor to negotiate with Gen. Tipton for the purchase of the battle ground land, consisting of about thirteen acres. On another page we reproduce an autograph letter written by Gov. Noble to Gen. Tipton asking him to sell the land to the state and on another page appears Tipton's reply in his own hand writing, offering to donate the ground. The conveyance of the gift is recorded in the Recorder's office at LaFayette. The records show that the transfer was made on November 7, 1836, the twenty-fifth anniversary of the famous battle. The record was lost and for several years there was a dispute over the title. Alva O. Reser, of LaFayette, became interested in the history of the battle and while preparing an address to be delivered before the Battle Ground Chautauqua he went to Logansport and by the assistance of a grand-daughter of Gen. Tipton, found the original letters neatly tied in a bundle and kept in an old trunk owned by her grand-father. Among these papers were documents that quieted the title to the battle grounds. On February 4, 1837, a year after the donation of the battle grounds, a resolution was passed by the Legislature instructing the Governor to offer a suitable premium for a design for a monument to be erected on the battlefield, pledging the faith of the state to complete the same. This promise, pledged seventy years ago, is still unfulfilled.

Gov. Noble went out of office in 1837 and after the death of Gen. Tipton in 1839, the project was forgotten. Even the ground was not taken care of, cattle roamed over the burial places of the heroic dead and their hallowed mounds were trampled upon. The historic oaks, showing bullet marks of the rifles were cut down in many instances, until, finally at the meeting of the Constitutional Convention of 1850, when on Saturday, December 21, John Pettit, a member of the Convention from Tippecanoe County, introduced a resolution to incorporate a section in the Constitution of the State, article 4, section 10, which reads as follows: "It shall be the duty of the General Assembly to provide for the permanent enclosure and preservation of the Tippecanoe Battlefield."

In 1873, sixty-two years after the battle was fought, an appropriation of $24,000 was made by the legislature to enclose the ground with an iron fence and to otherwise provide for the care of the grounds. Only $18,000 of the amount was expended and $6,000 reverted to the State Treasury. In 1837 an appropriation of $3,500 was made for painting the fence and other work. There is now in force a permanent appropriation calling for $300 a year to take care of the grounds, to be expended by the County Commissioners, a trust which is faithfully carried out. Congressman E. D. Crumpacker, from the Tenth District, introduced a bill in Congress asking for an appropriation of $25,000 for the purpose of erecting a monument to the memory of those whose bones are buried on this historic battlefield. By an earnest appeal he succeeded in getting the last session of Congress to make the appropriation and now, nearly a century since the battle was fought, a suitable monument is to be erected.

The battle ground is now the property of the state and surrounding it is a high iron fence. It is a beautiful grove of native forest trees and thousands of people assemble near by every year, attending the battle ground camp meetings. The writer of this book was there a little over a year ago with several hundred newspaper publishers from nearly every State in the Union. Nearly all of them knew of Gen. Harrison and of the great battle, but very few had ever heard of Gen. Tipton. Capt. DeHart and William R. Wood made short addresses, in which they told of the battle, pointing out the positions of the Indians, the place of attack and the spot where nearly two hundred American citizen soldiers fell for the advance of civilization.

The battle of Tippecanoe established Capt. Tipton's fame as an Indian fighter and he was regarded as a leader to be depended upon in those troubleous times when the Indian was a continuous menace to the constantly encroaching settlers.

The Indians were more or less troublesome during the years 1811 and 1812. They would assemble and invade settlements, killing men, women and children. On one occasion, in Scott County, a band of Shawnee Indians made a raid on a settlement on Pigeon Roost Creek. and killed every settler. It was one of the most atrocious, startling and cruel massacres ever chronicled in the annals of Indiana.

On September 3, 1812, J. Payne and a man named Coffman were out

Indianapolis Nov. 1st 1834

The Hon John Tipton

Sir

The last Legislature of our State, by a Joint Resolution, made it the duty of the Governor to ascertain the terms upon which, you would surrender the ground, on which was fought, the memorable Battle of Tippecanoe. With the events of that struggle honorable mention has been frequently made of your name, of your fellow officers and Soldiers who survived it by the brave General who commanded, as well as of those who were slain; and knowing your high estimate of the courage and private virtues of your companions who fell and whose remains render that a sacred spot, I need say but little to induce you to appreciate the motive which prompts the measure, that of a just regard for the memory of the lamented dead. Allow me to refer you to the resolution and request an answer as early as your convenience will permit.

I am Sir

With great esteem,

Your obt Servt

N. Noble

(Resolution to be found in last volume of our laws,)

Translation of Governor Noble's letter to Gen. Tipton, requesting terms upon which the Tippecanoe Battle Grounds could be purchased. See copy of original letter on opposite page.

Indianapolis, Nov. 1st, 1834.

The Hon. John Tipton,

Sir

The last legislature of our State, by a joint-resolution, made it the duty of the Governor to ascertain the terms upon which you would surrender the grounds on which was fought the memorable Battle of Tippecanoe. With the events of that struggle, honorable mention has been made of your name, of your fellow officers and soldiers who survived by the line General who commanded, as well of those who were slain, and knowing your high estimate of the courage and private virtues of your companions who fell and whose remains render that a sacred spot, I need say but little to induce you to appreciate the motive which prompts the measure that of a just regard for the memory of the lamented dead. Allow me to refer you to the resolution and request an answer as early as your convenience will permit

I am Sir
With Great Esteem
Your Obt. Svt.,
N. Noble.

(Resolution to be found in last volume of our laws.)

Falls of the wabash 7th Nov 1834

His Excy N Noble

Sir

I have the honour to acknowledge the receipt of your favour of the first of this month informing me that by a Resolution of the last Legislature ~~of this state~~ it was made the duty of the Governor to ascertain upon what terms I would surrender ~~convey~~ to the state the ground upon which was fought the memorable battle of Tippecanoe. and in reply I have to inform you that in purchasing the battle ground I was actuated by no other motive than that of possessing it ~~that ground~~ in order to preserve the bones of my companions in arms ~~brave~~ who fell there, and that it will afford me grate pleasure to convey the battleground to the state of Indiana, free of any charge, when ever it is signified to me that the state wishes it so conveyed ~~to her~~ for that purpose.

Translation of Gen. John Tipton's letter in answer to that of Governor Noble requesting terms upon which the Tippecanoe Battle Grounds could be purchased. See copy of original letter on opposite page.

Falls of the Wabash 7th of Nov. 1834.

His Excy N. Noble

Sir

I have the honor to acknowledge the receipt of your favor of the first of this month informing me that by a resolution of the last legislature it was made the duty of the Governor to asertain upon what terms I would surrender to the state the ground upon which was fought the memorable Battle of Tippecanoe, and in reply I have to inform you that in purchasing the battle ground I was actuated by no other motive than that of possessing it in order to preserve the bones of my companions in arms who fell there, and that it will afford me great pleasure to convey the battle ground to the State of Indiana, free of all charge, whenever it is signified to me that the State wishes it so conveyed for that purpose.

(Signed John Tipton.)

bee hunting in the woods and were surprised and killed by a band of twelve Indians. About sunset, on the same day, this party of Indians attacked the Pigeon Roost Settlement, and in the space of one hour, killed one man, five women and sixteen children. The bodies of some were burned in the fires which consumed the cabins. But one woman with three small children escaped the awful massacre. She walked all night and arrived at the home of a neighbor, several miles away, the next morning. The Indians followed her, but the man with whom she took refuge was prepared for them, and with his rifle, succeeded in driving them away. A company of Home Guards was organized and the country scoured for Indians, but they had gone so far away that the chase was abandoned. Gen. Tipton was notified and for several months he awaited the order to go to the rescue of the Settlements. The massacre of Pigeon Roost is of such historical importance that a few years ago the Legislature made an appropriation for the purpose of preserving the ground where it occurred. A well built fence surrounds the scene of the massacre and appropriate inscriptions mark the graves of those who were killed.

We find in Tipton's journal of 1812, an account of an expedition made to Driftwood Ford, of White River, where the Indians were giving the farmers much trouble. On the 30th day of June they sent a call to Gen. Tipton to come and drive the Red Men away. On July 5 he started with nine men, five more following in a few days. The next day they arrived at Fort Pleasant and on the evening of the same day they came upon Fort Defiance. The next day they divided their forces and scoured the country, but the Indians had heard that Capt. Tipton was after them, and knowing what kind of a Red Skin hunter he was, they stole away and never returned again. This expedition lasted in the neighborhood of twenty days.

The following year Capt. Tipton was promoted to the rank of Major and he was located at Fort Vallonia, near where Indians were committing many depredations. Tipton had under his command twenty-nine men, and on one of his scouting expeditions he met a party of Indians on an island in White river. He engaged them in battle and pressed the attack with such energy that the enemy fell back and were soon running for their lives, throwing their guns and blankets away, jumping into the river and swimming to the other shore. Several Indians were killed and wounded and a few more were drowned in attempting to swim across the river. Tipton lost no men killed or wounded.

Tipton was a disciplinarian. He enforced order and obedience and was not slow to punish any one who would disobey his command. During this engagement on the island he ordered that there must be no talking and that absolute silence must prevail. While creeping up onto the Indians, a great big fellow kept talking. Tipton went up to him, took his gun from him and tied him to a tree among the tall horse weeds. He could not move and bullets from the enemies guns whizzed near him, keeping him in constant fear and he was glad to promise to "be still." Tipton loosened the strings and he went to the front and fought like a hero. This battle is known to this day as the "Battle of Tipton's Island."

In the early part of 1813 Indians were still troublesome toward the north, and Tipton was sent to subdue them. In April, with thirty-one men, an engagement was had with the Indians in which two men were killed, however, the Indians were severely punished and began to make a rapid retreat. Then Gen. Tipton pushed forward, and on Salt River, now in Brown County, a running fight was kept up and there was more or less shooting every day. However, the Indians were severely punished and by the middle of the summer all signs of trouble disappeared.

It was in this year that peace was declared with Great Britain and no more trouble was apprehended and the people went to work to develop farms, build roads and locate towns. Emigrants flocked into the country and it was but a few years until all the wild Indian waste was brought under cultivation, and evidences of prosperity prevailed in all Southern Indiana. At the declaration of peace Tipton was promoted to the rank of Brigadier-General by President Monroe, and he returned to his home at Corydon, which city, had during his years of Indian warfare, become the seat of the Territorial Capital, it previously being located at Vincennes.

In 1816 Indiana became a state, the nineteenth territory to enter the Union. At the first election held in Harrison County John Tipton was elected Sheriff and he was re-elected. In the State election held in August, 1819, he was elected a Representative to the State Legislature, and to this office also received a re-election. On January 11, 1820, the Governor appointed a Commission, consisting of Tipton, George Hunt, John Conner, John Gilliland, Stephen Ludlow, Joseph Bartholomew, Jesse E. Durham, Frederick Rapp, William Prince and Thomas Emmerson, to select and locate a site for the new capital for the State. Vincenness, Corydon, Madison, Terre Haute, Vallonia, Strawtown, Indi-

GOVERNOR NOAH NOBLE.

anapolis and other towns were petitioners for the capital and the commissioners visited all of them. The merits and demerits, the advantages and disadvantages of all sites were carefully investigated. After a considerable time, the Commission met at Indianapolis to determine the site. The bids had narrowed down between Strawtown and Indianapolis, with a strong inclination toward Strawtown, due to the efforts of William Conner, then an influential citizen. General Tipton was favorable to Indianapolis and to head off further discussion and delay, he made a motion that Indianapolis be made the site of the new capital. Great excitement prevailed in this meeting, which took place in the home of John McCormick, the grand-father of Nicholas S. Martz, of Tipton. When the vote was cast and counted, Indianapolis was selected by a close margin.

In 1821 Tipton was appointed a Commissioner by the Legislature, with a like Commissioner from Illinois, to locate the boundary line between the two States. But for an error made by the surveyor, who failed to establish a true meridian, the great city of Chicago, would, today be in the State of Indiana instead of in the State of Illinois. Gen. Tipton insisted at the time that the territory comprising Cook County belonged to Indiana, but the surveyor's notes had a stronger influence than Tipton's argument, and Chicago was lost to Indiana.

It was during this period of the history of the State of Indiana that extensive improvements were inaugurated all over the United States. A great national road was being built through Indiana from Baltimore to St. Louis. During this session of the Legislature a public highway was conceived a hundred feet wide, running from Lake Michigan to the Ohio River. Gen. Tipton took great interest in these improvements and he was one of a Committee to negotiate with the Indians for a strip of ground through their reservations for the road. Evidences of this undertaking are still in existence, for in every town through which the road passed, the streets are one hundred feet wide. This accounts for the great width of the main street in Rochester and other towns along the old Michigan Road. At this time canals were also being constructed and Tipton was one of the prominent men who planned and had surveyed a number of canal routes, among them the Wabash and Erie Canal and the White-Water Canal near Richmond.

In 1823 Gen. Tipton was appointed Indian Agent by President Monroe for the Pottawatomie and Miami Indians. He was located at Fort Wayne, and made his home in the old block house, where he was at all times safe from attacks by the Indians. It was here in 1824 that Allen County was organized and at Gen. Tipton's suggestion the County was named in honor of Col. James Allen, of Kentucky, who was killed at the Indian massacre at the River Raisen. While he was performing his duties as Indian Agent the President appointed him, together with Gen. Lewis Cass, of Detroit, and Governor John B. Ray, to negotiate a treaty with the two tribes over which the General was agent. A treaty was made at Paradise Springs, on October 16, 1826, at the junction of the Mississiniwa and Wabash Rivers, by which the Indians ceded all the north-west part of Indiana to the government. This cession included a part of Tipton County, the reserve line running through the town of Tipton. After the treaty was made many of the Miamis, who lived on the border, and therefore were not present, became restless and dissatisfied. They did not understand the terms of the treaty and threatened trouble. David Foster, of Kokomo, did all he could to make them understand that the treaty was a fair one and that they should obey it and join in the great removal that was soon to take place. But they were stubborn and sullen. They could not give up their old hunting grounds. They had been so often deceived and disappointed that they thought that this meant their final extinction. The traditions of a long ancestry appealed to them and they were very bitter toward the Government and the Big Chiefs that consented to the treaty. To give them a better understanding of the nature of the treaty, upon the suggestion of David Foster, it was arranged that Gen. Tipton come and explain to them the conditions of the treaty. A day was set and a great barbacue planned. Hundreds of Indians assembled and a big dinner was served. Wild meats, corn bread and other luxuries of that day were spread upon the ground and Gen. Tipton and a few other white guests sat and ate with the Red Men. Gen. Tipton then spoke to the assembly. He succeeded in making the terms of the treaty plain and they were satisfied and when the day came for them to go to the far west they quietly submitted, not, however, without many regrets. Many tears were shed and more than once they turned and looked back, and with bowed heads bade "farewell, farewell, old, old, home."

Many years ago the writer had frequent talks with David Foster about the early settlement of this county, and as nearly as we can determine the place where the barbacue was held is in the field about a half mile north and west of Tipton, near the old Martz canning factory.

This practically ended all the Indian wars in Indiana, except in

1838, when trouble arose over the removal of the Pottawatomies from their reservation in Marshall County, near Twin Lake and the Yellow River, and then it was only by the timely arrival of Gen. Tipton that blood-shed was averted. Twenty-two sections of good and fertile land were especially reserved to the Pottawatomie Indians, presided over by four Chiefs, named Menominee, Pipinawa, Nakata and Macatawmaaw. Menominee was the oldest, a peaceable and pious Indian, always friendly to the whites. Early in life he forsook his pagan religion and became a Christian, joining the Catholic church under the guidance of Father Theodore Badin, who was the first Catholic Priest ordained in the United States. In 1828 a Chapel was erected with an upstairs room where the Priest resided. A little village grew up around it and an effort made to agriculture.

The reservation was in the path of the proposed Michigan road and frequent efforts had been made by the whites to get possession of it, and by continued bartering they succeeded in getting the three younger Chiefs, made stupid with drink, to sign their rights away. These three received 14,080 silver dollars for their share. Menominee did not sign the treaty, nor did he ever sign it. By the terms of the treaty, the entire tribe was to be removed to the Osage country, west of the Missouri River and the 6th day of August, 1838, was the date fixed for their departure. As the day approached the Indians became restless and there were mutterings and resistance threatened. To make matters worse and to precipitate a conflict, a squatter named Waters, settled on the reservation. This so enraged the Indians that in the dead hour of night they made an attack on his cabin and chopped the door down, but were driven away without the shedding of blood. A report of threatened trouble was made to Gov. Wallace, who rode all the way from Indianapolis to Twin Lake on horse back to investigate. It was evident to him that there would be an outbreak among the Indians unless they were overawed by soldiers, so he called Gen. Tipton. With one hundred soldiers, Tipton arrived at the little village, finding nearly all the Indians near the Chapel attending worship and listening to the counsel of the good and wise Chief Menominee. Tipton carried out his instructions and the poor, oppressed Indians were surrounded and overpowered. Dejected and humiliated, they were forced to obey. General Tipton, Abel C. Pepper, the Government Indian Agent, and the Catholic Priest, Father Petit, counseled peace and a consent to their removal.

VIEW OF BATTLEGROUND FROM THE NORTHEAST.

In answer to their argument, Chief Menominee made the following speech:

> "Your President, he does not know the truth. He does not know Menominee did not sign the land away. He does not know Menominee's people want to be peaceable and do not want the whiskey of the white man. He does not know the Young Chiefs were drunk and foolish when they signed the land away. Your Chief, the President, is a good man, and if he could know the truth he would not take Menominee away from his home, tied like a dog. He has not heard the counsel of the wise Chiefs. He has heard only the young Chiefs."

With that he sat down and the silence that followed was oppressive. Finally, he arose, passed the "pipe of peace" to General Tipton and counseled the tribe to obey the mandates of the white man. On September 4, 1838, General Tipton started to the far west with 859 men, women and children. Before leaving the tribe went to the graves of their fathers where they wailed piteously. An old French woman, seventy-two years old, was their only friend that gave them comfort and consolation. Her sympathies reconciled them and in her presence they kissed the cross and made ready for the long journey. The women, children, the old and infirm were put in big Government wagons and the start was made, single file. It was a sad and sorrowful sight, like a funeral procession. Not a word was spoken, each being sullen, crestfallen and heartbroken. On the way 156 died of chills, fevers and malarial diseases. A few years later Menominee died of a broken heart. This was the last of the Pottawatomies in Indiana.

This is the sad side of the Indian story and it creates a feeling, that after all, the Indian was not so much to blame for his savagery, when his home, his land and his hunting ground were taken from him, sometimes honestly and sometimes dishonestly. At the session of the Legislature, in 1907, Hon. Daniel McDonald, of Plymouth, succeeded in getting a bill passed, appropriating $2,500 for the purpose of restoring the old Mission Church and the erection of a monument to the memory of the good pious old Indian Chief, Menominee.

In all the Indian wars, General Tipton was foremost in all contests, and while he had a bitter hatred for the Indian and was ready to take arms any time against them, he always fought them fair. He never killed an Indian because he was an Indian, but he fought them in a cause that demanded the possession of a country for a civilized and progressive race. His removal of the Pottawatomies is the only evidence of cruelty, however, he was acting under orders and the sufferings of the deported tribe were unavoidable. It was the only season of the year that they could be removed with as little exposure as possible and, perhaps, they fared better than they would had the removal taken place earlier or later in the season.

In the spring of 1828 General Tipton moved the Indian agency from Fort Wayne to the "Mouth of Eel River," near the junction with the Wabash, where the town of Logansport had just been surveyed. The town had not been named and Tipton suggested that it bear the name of "Mouth of Eel River." Other names were suggested, one of them being in honor of the great Indian Chief Logan, who had been friendly to the whites throughout all the Indian wars. To arbitrate the matter it was decided that Tipton and Col. Duret should shoot at a mark, and the one coming nearest to it, four shots out of seven, was to have the honor. Duret won by coming nearest the mark four times, therefore the town was named Logan. The suffix, "port," was afterward affixed, making it "Logansport."

On February 26, 1831, Gen. James Noble, a United States Senator from Indiana, died in Washington. Tipton's name was vigorously advocated to fill the vacancy, but Gov. Ray appointed Hon. Robert Hanna, who served until the meeting of the next Legislature, when Tipton was elected in spite of the efforts to elect Hanna. At the next session Tipton was elected Senator to serve a full term of six years. While in the Senate he became a fast friend of President Andrew Jackson, and upon more than one occasion, he was the President's guest at the Hermitage, in Tennessee. This friendship continued until the question of the renewal of the charter of the United States Bank. Tipton was in favor of the re-chartering of the banks, while the President bitterly opposed it. Tipton argued hard, for he believed that the renewal of the charter would be of great advantage to the new States in the west. The bill passed, but when it went to the President, he vetoed it, thus ending one of the bitterest contests in Congress on financial questions.

The President of the Senate appointed Tipton Chairman of the Committee of Indian Affairs and it was he and Oliver H. Smith who procured the passage of a bill to purchase the Miami Indian Reserve, making it possible for Tipton County to be organized and become a part of the great State of Indiana. In a volume of biographical sketches of United States Senators, among the archives now in Washington, appears the following: "John Tipton, the subject of this sketch, has been noticed as the Ensign hero of Capt. Spencer's company at the battle of Tippecanoe. He is of medium height, well set, short face, round head, low wrinkled forehead, sunken gray eyes, stern countenance, good chest, stiff sandy hair, standing erect from his forehead. He is the Chairman of the Committee of Indian Affairs, a position he is eminently qualified for, having been for many years Indian Agent and well acquainted with most of the western tribes. He is a man of great energy and character, is a most faithful Senator, always in his seat ready to vote. He is not what is called an eloquent debater, still he is plain and strong as a speaker. He sees a question clearly and marches directly at it without rhetorical flourishes."

After his retirement from the United States Senate Tipton refused a re-election, his life had been a busy and strenuous one, and he had a desire to return to private life. He believed in Indiana soil and at different times owned land in Harrison, Bartholomew, Allen, Huntington, Cass and Tippecanoe Counties. He, jointly with Col. Duret, his brother-in-law, entered a large tract of land between Eel and Wabash Rivers, the present site of the City of Logansport. He became deeply interested in educational affairs and donated ground for school purposes, the effect still being felt in that thriving City. He donated property to the order of Free Masons and to churches and other public institutions. In addition to these gifts he was liberal in all the towns in which he was interested. He donated ground on which the battle of Tippecanoe was fought to the state. He donated thirty acres of ground to Columbus, the County Seat of Bartholomew County. He gave freely to Fort Wayne, Huntington and Logansport. He built a dam across Eel River at Logansport, which is still in existence, and made many other gifts for benevolent and educational purposes.

General Tipton was also prominent in the Masonic order in Indiana. In 1817 he received the Master Masons degree at Corydon and the next year he was a Representative to the Grand Lodge, held January 12, 1818, at Madison. He was elected Senior Warden, being the first man in the State to hold that office. In 1819 he was elected Deputy Grand Master and in 1820 was elected Grand Master, at Jeffersonville. Upon his removal to Fort Wayne he proceeded to organize a lodge of Masons there, the first meeting being held in his room at the fort. When the lodge was organized he was elected its first Senior Warden. He was again made a Representative to the grand lodge, which met at Indianapolis and was again elected Grand Master. Upon his removal to Logansport, in 1828, he immediately organized a lodge of Masons and in his honor, the lodge was named Tipton lodge, No. 33. Again he was a Representative to the Grand Lodge. He was also a Royal Arch Mason, having taken the degree at Louisville in 1827.

General Tipton was twice married. His first wife was his cousin, Miss Jennie Shields, daughter of John Shields, who became famous in the Lewis and Clark Expedition. She was the mother of two sons, one being Spier S. Tipton, who became a graduate of West Point, and a Captain of Dragoons in the Mexican war, and who died in Mexico shortly after peace was declared.

The second wife of General Tipton was Miss Matilda Spencer, a daughter of his old neighbor and commander, who fell in the battle of Tippecanoe. Three children were born to the last marriage, George, John and Hariett. George, who managed his father's estate, died in Logansport. John, a graduate of West Point, died in California at the beginning of the rebellion, a Captain in the United States Army, and Hariett, who married Thomas S. Dumont, of Logansport, died soon after the Civil War in Oregon.

On February 14, 1839, Mrs. Matilda Tipton, wife of General John Tipton, died and on April 4, less than two months afterward, her husband died after a very brief illness. While superintending a proposed improvement of his extensive water privileges he contracted a severe cold from exposure, and on the next day, after a few hours of unconscious suffering, he died. He was buried at Logansport on Sunday, April 7, 1839, with military honors and the rites of the Masonic order.

Thus ended an eventful, busy, useful and honorable life. In his early childhood he realized that there were great possibilities and with that energy that marked his entire career he succeeded in whatever he undertook. He never forgot those who were in arms against the Indians with him and his respect for his dead comrades was so strong that when a new county was organized he urged that it be named for one of them. His appeal was often listened too and as a result the counties of Floyd, Posey, Scott, Warrick, Spencer, Wells, Daviess,

Parke, Harrison and Bartholomew were named for men who were engaged in the battle of Tippecanoe. He was so unselfish that he never asked that any county be named for himself and it was never suggested during his life. The nearest he came to having his name perpetuated was when he donated thirty acres of ground to Bartholomew County for a County Seat, with the understanding that the town be named "Tiptona," but for political reasons the name was changed to Columbus. Tipton was very much chagrinned over the change and lost interest in his town, and it is said that he never visited it again. Rather than pass through it, in going from one place to another, he would make a detour around it.

Five years after his death, Tipton County was organized, and some one who knew the General suggested that his name be honored and perpetuated by naming the new County Tipton. Thus is was that after he had passed from an eventful career, he was honored by the naming of a County and City to his memory. The citizens of Tipton and Tipton County are proud of the name. They honor him for whom it was named and, now, seventy years after his death, it is proposed to erect a monument that future generations may know that a "history maker, an Indian fighter, and a public spirited citizen," helped to make it possible that the Great Central Northwest developed into the richest and most prosperous section of country in the entire Union. It is proper that the citizens of Tipton County take cognizance of this and commemorate the name of General John Tipton by the erection of a suitable monument to his memory. It is a spirit of patriotism and a recognition of the value of men to the country and welfare of all the people.

A Letter Written by a Tippecanoe Battle Hero.

The writer of this work had the good fortune to secure a copy of a letter written by Judge Isaac Naylor, of Crawfordsville, who died in 1873. The Judge was in the battle of Tippecanoe and, also, was one of the first to arrive at the Pigeon Roost massacre after the Indians had left. Mr. M. W. Phillips, of LaFayette, who is devoting a good deal of time and energy to hunting up facts and traditions of the early history of the state, recently met a daughter of the Judge, and by her permission he looked over many letters filed away by the old warrior. Among the pile of letters, he happened to find one giving a clear, vivid and interesting account of incidents connected with this memorable march up the Wabash and the battle of Tippecanoe. It is through the kindness of Mr. Phillips that we are able to re-produce it in this volume:

"I became a volunteer member of a company of riflemen and, on the twelfth of September, 1811, we commenced our march toward Vincennes, and arrived there in about six days, marching 120 miles. We remained there about a week and took up the march to a point on the Wabash river sixty miles above, on the east bank of the river, where we erected a stockade fort, which he named Fort Harrison. This was three miles below where the City of Terre Haute now stands. Col. Joseph H. Daviess, who commanded the dragoons, named the fort. The glorious defense of this fort nine months after by Captain Zachariah Taylor was the first step in his brilliant career that afterward made him President of the United States. A few days later we took up the march again for the seat of Indian warfare, where we arrived on the evening of November 6, 1811.

"When the army arrived in view of Prophet's Town, an Indian was seen coming toward General Harrison, with a white flag suspended on a pole. Here the army halted, and a parley was had between General Harrison and an Indian delegation, who assured the General that they desired peace and solemnly promised to meet him the next day in council to settle the terms of peace and friendship between them and the United States.

"General Marston G. Clark, who was then Brigade Major, and Walter Taylor, and one of the Judges of the General Court of the Territory of Indiana, and afterward a Senator of the United States of Indiana, (one of the General's aides) were ordered to select a place for the encampment, which they did. The army then marched to the ground selected about sunset. A strong guard was placed around the encampment commanded by Capt. James Bigger, and three lieutenants. The troops were ordered to sleep on their arms. The night being cold, large fires were made along the lines of the encampment and each soldier retired to rest, sleeping on his arms.

"Having seen a number of squaws and children at the town, I thought the Indians were not disposed to fight. About 10 o'clock at night Joseph Warnock and myself retired to rest, he taking one side of the fire and I the other. The other members of our company being all asleep. My friend Warnock dreamed the night before, a bad dream, which foreboded something fatal to him, or to some of his family, as he told me. Having myself no confidence in dreams, I thought little about the matter, although I observed that he never smiled afterward.

"I awoke about 4 o'clock the next morning, after a sound and refreshing sleep, having heard in a dream the firing of guns and the whistling of bullets just before I awoke from my slumbers. A drizzling rain was falling and all things were still and quiet throughout the camp. I was engaged in making a calculation when I should arrive at home.

"In a few moments I heard the crack of a rifle in the direction of the point where now stands the Battle Ground House, which is occupied by Captain DuTiel as a tavern. I had just time to think that some sentinel was alarmed and had fired his rifle without a real cause, when I heard the crack of another rifle, followed by an awful Indian yell all around the encampment. In less than a minute I saw the Indians charging our line most furiously and shooting a great many rifle balls into our camp fires, throwing the live coals into the air three or four feet high.

"At this moment my friend Warnock was shot by a rifle ball through his body. He ran a few yards and fell dead on the ground. Our lines were broken and a few Indians were found on the inside of the encampment. In a few moments they were all killed. Our lines closed up and our men in their proper places. One Indian was killed in the back part of Captain Geiger's tent, while he was attempting to tomahawk the Captain.

"The sentinels, closely pursued by the Indians, came to the lines of the encampment in haste and confusion. My brother, William Naylor, was on guard. He was pursued so rapidly and furiously that he ran to the nearest point on the left flank, where he remained with a company of regular soldiers until the battle was near its termination. A young man, whose name was Daniel Pettit, was pursued so closely and furiously by an Indian as he was running from the guard fire to our lines, that to save his life he cocked his rifle as he ran and turning suddenly round, placed the muzzle of his gun against the body of the Indian and shot an ounce ball through him. The Indian fired his gun at the same instant, but it being longer than Pettit's the muzzle passed by him and set fire to a handkerchief which he had tied around his head.

"The Indians made four or five most fierce charges on our lines, yelling and screaming as they advanced, shooting balls and arrows into our ranks. At each charge they were driven back in confusion, carrying off their dead and wounded as they retreated.

"Colonel Owen, of Shelby County, Kentucky, one of General Harrison's volunteer aides fell early in action by the side of the General. He was a member of the Legislature at the time of his death. Colonel Daviess was mortally wounded early in the battle, gallantly charging the Indians on foot with his sword and pistols, according to his own request. He made this request three times of General Harrison, before he permitted him to make the charge. This charge was made by himself and eight dragoons on foot near the angle formed by the left flank and front line of the encampment.

"Colonel Daviess lived about thirty-six hours after he was wounded; manifesting his ruling passions in life, ambition, patriotism and an ardent love of military glory. During the last hours of his life he said to his friends around him, that he had but one thing to regret, that he had military talents; that he was about to be cut down in the meridian of life without having an opportunity to display them for his own honor and the good of his country. He was buried alone with the honors of war near the right flank of the army, inside of the lines of the encampment, between two trees. On one of these trees the letter "D" is now visible. Nothing but the stump of the other remains. His grave was made here to conceal it from the Indians. It was filled up to the top with earth and then covered with oak leaves. I presume the Indians never found it. This precautionary act was performed as a mark of peculiar respect for a distinguished hero and patriot of Kentucky.

"Captain Spencer's company of mounted riflemen, composed the right flank of the army. Captain Spencer and both his Lieutenants were killed. John Tipton was elected and commissioned as Captain of this Company in one hour after the battle, as a reward for his cool and deliberate heroism displayed during the action. He died at Logansport in 1839, having been twice elected Senator of the United States from the State of Indiana.

"The clear and calm voice of General Harrison was heard in words of heroism in every part of the encampment, during the action. Colonel Boyd behaved very bravely after repeating these words: 'Huzza! My sons of gold, a few more fires and victory will be ours!'

"Just after daylight the Indians retreated across the prairie toward their town, carrying off their wounded. This retreat was from the right flank of the encampment, composed of two rifle companies, commanded by Captains Spencer and Robb, having retreated from the other portions of the encampment a few minutes before. As their retreat became visible, an almost universal shout was raised by our men. 'Huzza! Huzza! Huzza!' This shout was nearly equal to that of the savages at the commencement of the battle, ours was the shout of victory, theirs was the shout of ferocious, but disappointed hope.

"The morning light disclosed the fact that the killed and wounded of our army, numbering between eight and nine hundred men, amounted to one hundred and eighty. Thirty-six Indians were found dead near our lines. Many of their dead were carried off during the battle. This fact was proved by the discovery of many Indian graves recently made near their town. Ours was a bloody victory, theirs a bloody defeat.

"Soon after breakfast an Indian Chief was discovered on the prairie, about eighty yards from our front line, wrapped in a piece of white cloth. He was found by a soldier by the name of Miller, a resident of Jeffersonville, Indiana. The Indian was wounded in one of his legs, the ball having penetrated his knee and passed down his leg, breaking the bone as it passed. Miller put his foot against him and he raised up his head and said: 'Don't kill me, don't kill me.' At the same time five or six regular soldiers tried to shoot him, but their muskets snapped and missed fire. Major Davis Floyd came riding toward him with dragoon sword and pistols and said he 'would show then how to kill Indians,'* when a messager came from General Harrison, commanding that he should be taken prisoner. He was taken into the camp, where the surgeons dressed his wounds. Here he refused to speak a word of English or tell a word of truth. Through the medium of an interpreter he said that he was a friend to the white people and that the Indians shot him, while he was coming to the camp to tell General Harrison that they were about to attack the army. He refused to have his leg amputated, though he was told that amputation was the only means of saving his life. One dogma of Indian superstition is that all good and brave Indians, when they die, go to a delightful region, abounding with deer and other game, and that to be a successful hunter, he should have all his limbs, his gun and his dog. He therefore preferred death with all his limbs to life without them. In accordance with his request he was left to die, in company with an old squaw, who was found in the Indian town the next day after he was taken prisoner. They were left in one of our tents.

"At the time this Indian was taken prisoner, another Indian, who was wounded in the body, rose to his feet in the middle of the prairie, and began to walk toward the woods on the opposite side. A number of regular soldiers shot at him and missed him. A man who was a member of the same company with me, Henry Huckleberry, ran a few steps into the prairie and shot an ounce rifle ball through his body and he fell dead near the margin of the woods. Some Kentucky volunteers went across the prairie immediately and scalped him, dividing his scalp into four pieces. Each one cutting a hole in each piece, putting his ramrod through the hole, and placing his part of the scalp just behind the first thimble of his gun, near its muzzle. Such was the fate of nearly all the Indians found dead on the battle ground, and such was the disposition of their scalps.

"The death of Owen, and the fact that Daviess was mortally wounded, with the remembrance also that a large portion of Kentucky's best blood had been shed by the Indians, must be their apology for this barbarous conduct. Such conduct will be excused by all who witnessed the bloody scenes of this battle.

"Tecumseh being absent at the time of battle, a chief called White Loon, was the chief commander of the Indians. He was seen in the morning after the battle, riding a large white horse in the woods across the prairie, where he was shot at by a volunteer named Montgomery, who is now living in the southwest part of this State. At the crack of his rifle the horse jumped as if the ball had hit him. The Indian rode off toward the town and we saw him no more. During the battle the Prophet was safely located on a hill, beyond the reach of our balls, praying to the Great Spirit to give the victory to the Indians. Having previously assured them that the Great Spirit would change our powder into ashes and sand.

"We had about forty head of beef cattle when we came to the battle ground. They all ran off the night of the battle, or they were driven off by the Indians, so that they were all lost. We received rations for two days on the morning after the battle. We received no more rations until the next Tuesday evening, being six days afterward. The Indians having retreated to their town, we performed the solemn duty of consigning to their graves our dead soldiers, without shrouds or coffins. They were placed in graves about two feet deep, from five to ten in each grave.

"General Harrison having learned that Tecumseh was expected to return from the south with a number of Indians whom he had enlisted in his cause, called a council of his officers, who advised him to remain on the battlefield and fortify his camp by a breastwork of logs around, about four feet high. This work was completed during the day and all the troops were placed immediately behind each line of the work when they were ordered to pass the watchword from right to left every five minutes, so that no man was permitted to sleep during the night. The watchword was 'Wide awake,' 'Wide awake.' To me it was a long, cold, cheerless night.

"On the next day the dragoons went to Prophet's Town, which they found deserted by all the Indians, except an old squaw, whom they brought into the camp and left her with the wounded chief before mentioned. The dragoons set fire to the town and it was all consumed, casting up a brilliant light amid the darkness of the ensuing night. I arrived at the town when it was about half on fire. I found large quantities of corn, beans and peas. I filled my knapsack with these articles and carried them to the camp and divided them with the members of our mess, cconsisting of six men. Having these articles of food we declined eating horse flesh which was eaten by a large portion of our men."

TECUMSEH.

Life of Tecumseh Kamskaka.

It was Tecumseh and the Prophet, his brother, that fomented trouble between the Indians and the white settlers throughout Indiana. Nearly all the other Indian nations were disposed to become friendly, but by the intrigue of the British government, the Indians were slow to obey the mandates of the American government. The war of 1812 was brewing and it was the policy of Great Britain to cause as much unrest among the Indians in the west as possible, to make it all the more possible for them to carry on war in the east. Great Britain found a great friend in Tecumseh and it took a bloody battle and a humilating defeat to convince the Indians that they could not assist England, maintain their tribal relations and hold possession of so rich a country as Indiana. It is not certain that the warrior Tecumseh was in the battle of Tippecanoe, (for there is no evidence that he was near.) Some writers have said that had he been there, results would have been quite different. Perhaps it would be of interest to produce, in connection with the life of General Tipton, a biographical sketch of the lives of these two noted Indian Chiefs.

Tecumseh Kamskaka, (signifying a wildcat springing on its prey,) was born of Shawnee parentage, at Old Piqua, near Springfield, Ohio, and was one of the boldest and most active of the braves who opposed Mad Anthony Wayne in 1794-95 and was at the treaty at Greenville. As early as 1804, he had begun the execution of a scheme in connection with his brother, "The Prophet," for confederating the western Indians for the purpose of exterminating the white people. He visited many tribes with his brother, who pretended to be a Commissioner from the Great Spirit. He was partially successful, when his plans were defeated by General Harrison at the battle of Tippecanoe. He next sought an alliance with the Seminoles, in Florida, the Creeks, in Alabama and Georgia, and tribes in Missouri. Not meeting with success, he returned to Indiana. In the fall of the same year, together with his brother, "The Prophet," he made another trip to the south. He took his brother with him, partly to employ him as a cunning instrument in managing the superstitious Indians, and partly to prevent his doing mischief at home in Tecumseh's absence. About thirty warriors accompanied them. His mission was to engage the barbarians as allies for the British and against the colonists. The Choctaws and Chickasaws, through whose country Tecumseh passed, would not listen to him, but the Seminoles and Creeks lent him willing ears. He addressed the Creeks for the first time in the lower part of Alabama, late in October. Soon afterward, having addressed the Creeks at different points, he approached a great council called by a United States Indian Agent, at Toockabatcha, the ancient Creek capital, where fully 5,000 of the barbarian nations were gathered. Tecumseh marched with dignity into the square with his train of thirty followers, entirely naked, excepting their flaps and ornaments, their faces painted black, their heads adorned with eagles' feathers, while buffalo tails dragged behind, suspended by bands around the waists. Like appendages were attached to their arms, and their whole appearance was as hidious as possible, while their bearing was uncommonly pompous and ceremonious. They marched round and round in the square, and then approached the Creek Chiefs, gave them the Indian salutation of a handshake at arm's length and exchanged tobacco in token of friendship. They kept up this pretense daily until the Indian Agent departed. That night a council was held in the great round house. It was packed with eager listeners. Tecumseh made a firery and vengeful speech, exhorting the Creeks to abandon the customs of the pale faces and return to those of their fathers for it was unworthy not to follow the footsteps of the noble hunter and warrior. He warned them that the whites were seeking to exterminate them and possess their country, and he told them that their friends, the British, had sent him from the Great Lake to invite them to the war path. The wily Prophet, who had been told by the British when a comet would appear, told the excited multitude that they would see the arm of Tecumseh, like pale fire, stretched out in the vault of Heaven at a certain time, and thus they would know by that sign when to begin the war. The people looked upon him with awe, for the fame of Tecumseh and the Prophet had preceeded them. Tecumseh continued his mission with partial success, however, he met with opposition here and there. Among the most conspicuous of the opposition was Tustinuggee-Thlucco, the Big Creek Warrior. Tecumseh tried every art to convert this big chief to his purpose. At length he said, "Tustinuggee-Thlucco, your blood is white. You have taken my redsticks and my talk, but you do not mean to fight. I know the reason, you do not believe the Great Spirit has sent me. You shall believe it. I will leave directly and go straight to Detroit. When I get there, I will stamp my foot upon the ground and shake down every house in Toockabatcha." Strangely enough, at about the time Tecumseh must have arrived at Detroit, there was heard a deep rumbling under ground all over the Alabama region, and there was a heaving of the earth that made the houses of Toockabatcha reel and totter as if about to fall. The startled savages ran out, exclaiming "Tecumseh is at Detroit! Tecumseh is at Detroit! We feel the stamp of his foot!" It was the shock of an earthquake that was felt all over the gulf region. At the same time, the comet, "the blazing arm of Tecumseh," appeared in the sky. These events made a powerful impression on nearly the whole Creek nation, but it did not move the "Big Warrior" from his alligeance to the United States. The Creeks, however, rose in arms, and in less than two years their nation was ruined. Tecumseh's visit brought dreadful calamity upon them.

After being driven out of Indiana, Tecumseh joined the British army and was commissioned a Brigadier-General. He was killed at the battle of Thames, in Canada, October 5, 1813. It is supposed that his slayer was Col. Richard M. Johnson, of Kentucky, who was afterward a candidate for Vice-President of the United States.

It was not long before his death, when his glory was at its heighth and he was meting out revenge on the Americans, that Commodore Perry fought the great battle of Put-inBay, the report of which coined the famous phrase, "We have met the enemy and they are ours." At one time during this great battle of the lakes, the British were gaining an advantage and were hurling shot thick and fast into Perry's flagship. It appeared that it would sink, when Perry jumped to the flagstaff and in full view of the British guns, cried out, "Don't give up the ship." Each man vied with the other to do his best and soon the British began to show signs of weakening and when the American ships pressed upon them, they hoisted the white flag, the battle was over and the Stars and Stripes waved from the topmost mast, signalling "victory" to all the world. Two ships, two brigs, one schooner and one sloop were captured and others went to the bottom of the lake. The result of this had a depressing effect upon Tecumseh and he resolved that he would never surrender nor give himself up to the Americans and when he saw fate staring him in the face he boldly stood before the sword of a Kentucky Colonel and allowed himself to be cut to his death.

THE PROPHET.

Life of The Prophet Elkswatawa.

The Prophet was also born near Piqua, Ohio, and in his early life was a worthless, drunken vagabond. He was ugly, quarrelsome and lazy. In a fight with a neighbor Indian, he lost an eye, an accident which ever afterward gave him a hidious appearance. This deformity he turned to account and used his bad eye to frighten the impressionable and superstitious. As early as 1805 he pretended to be supernaturally guided. He assumed the character of a "Medicine Man," and claimed to be directed by the Great Spirit. He cleverly began his scheme by falling suddenly one night while lighting his pipe, and laying apparently dead until he was borne away for burial. Then he opened his eye and said: "Be not fearful, I have been in the land of the Blessed. Call the nation together, that I may tell them what I have seen and heard." An assembly was summoned and he told a marvelous story of the land he had seen and the instructions and warning he had received. From that time he was a preacher and was called "The Prophet." So great was his influence that his disciples believed he possessed many of the powers of the Great Spirit. He told wonderful tales of his doings, saying that he could make pumpkins as large as wigwams spring from the ground, and corn so large that one ear would feed a dozen men. So great was his fame at one time, that the southern shores of Lake Superior and Michigan were almost depopulated and traders were compelled to abandon business, such throngs flocked to hear The Prophet. Not more than one-third of the deluded fanatics returned, the greater part having perished of hunger, cold and fatigue.

On the evening before the battle of Tippecanoe, after having promised General Harrison to give an answer the next morning as to accepting terms of peace, he surrounded himself with his dupes and prepared for treachery and murder. He brought out a pretended magic bowl. In one hand he held a "sacred torch," in the other a string of "holy beans," which was accounted miraculous in their effects. His followers were all required to touch this talisman and be made proof against harm and the white man's bullets, and then to take an oath to exterminate the pale faces. When this was accomplished The Prophet went through a long series of incantations and mysterious movements. He danced around the fire, appearing to be in intense agony, groaning and wreathing and twisting himself into all kinds of contortions. Then turning to his highly excited band, about 700 altogether, he told them that the time to attack the white man had come. "They are in your power," he said, holding up the holy beans as a reminder of their oaths. "They sleep now and never will wake. The Great Spirit will give light to us and darkness to the white man. Their bullets shall not harm us, your weapons shall be always fatal." Then followed war songs and dances, until the Indians, wrought up to a perfect frenzy, rushed forth to attack Harrison's camp without a leader. It was these orgies that Ensign Tipton heard while standing guard and he gave the alarm that the Indians were upon the camp. Stealthily the treacherous Indians crept through the long grass of the prairie in the deep gloom, intending to surround their enemy's position, kill the sentinels, rush into camp and massacre every one. The story of the battle is too well known to repeat here, but the result caused the Indians to doubt The Prophets inspirations by the Great Spirit. When he cunningly told them that his predictions concerning the battle had failed because his wife had touched the sacred vessels and broke the charm, they cursed him with reproaches. Even Indian superstition could not accept that flimsy falsehood for an excuse, and The Prophet was deserted by his disappointed followers and he was compelled to seek refuge among the Wyandottes. His power and influence were gone and he went to Canada where he died a miserable death.

Events Leading Up to The Battle of Tippecanoe.

August 20, 1794.—Battle of the Maumee Rapids, where General Anthony Wayne disastrously defeated the united Indian tribes. In this battle Harrison, serving as aid to General Wayne, first met in combat the young chief Tecumseh, who led the Shawnee Indians.

August 3, 1795.—Treaty at Greenville, Ohio, between Wayne and eleven Indian chiefs, ceding to the United States the disputed lands in the Maumee River Valley. Tecumseh refused to attend the council and never recognized the terms of the treaty.

1795-1801.—Wm. H. Harrison made Captain in 1795; secretary of the North-West Territory in 1798; delegate from that territory to Congress in 1799; and governor of the newly formed Territory of Indiana in 1801.

1803-'05.—Treaty between Harrison and the Indians.

1804-'05.—British agents inciting northwestern Indians to enmity against the Americans.

1805.—The Shawnee chief, Tecumseh, and his brother, The Prophet began the formation of the confederation of western Indian tribes for the recovery of their lost domain. The Prophet claimed to represent the Great Spirit and wielded a powerful religious influence on the Indians of various tribes, while Tecumseh moved from tribe to tribe from the Great Lakes to the Gulf, advocating the principle that the Indians were one people and that the lands being common property could not be sold by one tribe without the consent of all.

Spring of 1808.—By invitation of the Kickapoos and Pottawatomies Tecumseh and The Prophet removed with their tribe of Shawnees to the junction of the Tippecanoe and Wabash rivers where Prophet's Town was built and the headquarters of the Indian confederacy established.

August, 1808.—The Prophet visited Governor Harrison at Vincennes and disclaimed evil intentions in his influence over the Indian tribes of the west.

September 30, 1809.—Treaty at Fort Wayne in which Harrison purchased from the assembled chiefs title to two large bodies of land. Tecumseh was absent when this treaty was made and on his return protested against the validity of the sale, even threatening with death some of the chiefs who took part in the council.

July, 1810.—Harrison sent a conciliatory message to The Prophet at Prophet's Town.

August 12-22, 1810.—Tecumseh visited Governor Harrison at Vincennes accompanied by seventy-five armed Indians. Frequent interviews were held in which Tecumseh protested against the sale of lands at the last council at Fort Wayne. He openly told the governor of the powerful confederation he was forming, and of an intended visit to the British while on a trip to the Huron tribe. The conference on August 20 nearly ended in open hostility.

1810-'11.—Numerous minor attacks were made on settlers, who retaliated. Early in 1811 the British Agent of Indian Affairs took active steps to incite the northwestern Indians to discontent. In June, 1811, Harrison sent a warning message to Tecumseh at Prophet's Town. and on July 27, Tecumseh appeared at Vincennes, accompanied by a considerable band of Indians, enroute to southern tribes to complete his confederation. Anticipating this visit, the Governor had a review of the militia, numbering about 750 men. Tecumseh soon left for the south, and Harrison understanding that he would return in three months time, determined to move at once on the Indians at Prophet's Town and strike a blow at the confederation.

October 7, 1811.—The blow was struck, the Battle of Tippecanoe was fought, won and the Four Great North-West Territories saved from the British. It was in this battle that the fame of Ensign John Tipton became noted as a warrior and an Indian fighter.